THE BIASES OF THE ELEPHANT AGAINST THE LION AND LEOPARD

FUSHEINI YAKUBU

WORKBOOK PRESS LLC
187 E Warm Springs Rd,
Suite B285, Las Vegas, NV 89119, USA

Website: https://workbookpress.com/
Hotline: 1-888-818-4856
Email: admin@workbookpress.com

Ordering Information:
Quantity sales. Special discounts are available on quantity purchases by corporations, associations, and others.
For details, contact the publisher at the address above.

Library of Congress Control Number:
ISBN-13:   978-1-957618-56-2 (Paperback Version)
              978-1-957618-57-9 (Digital Version)

REV. DATE: 02/04/2022

THE BIASES OF THE ELEPHANT AGAINST THE LION AND LEOPARD

FUSHEINI YAKUBU

TABLE OF CONTENTS

ACKNOWLEDGEMENT.

"Better late than never". This is a wise saying that reveals the reason for writing this book. Some people may be endowed with some special talents, which may be hidden. When such people are touched by some events to use the talents, the impact almost becomes beneficial to others. It is in this light I found myself.

Though I am related to the legend's family of Bimbilla, the talent would have been lost if I was not moved to act by some people. To be precise, I met my grandfather, Alhaji Abdulai who is the Chief Legend of Bimbilla (Lung-Naa). He showered on me oral tradition that has been passed on from our Great Grandfathers, from the reign of Naa Gbewaa to the current Kingdom of the three main Gbewaa Kingdoms (Dagbon, Mamprugu and Nanung).

The current chieftaincy crisis has chopped into the moral fiber of the society, causing us to lose or distort the oral tradition. I thought it prudent to document this enviable oral tradition in a form of a book that could be used as a reference point for the new generation. As a leader of an organization that cares for the youth, I am much particular about socio-cultural issues that will affect the youth and generations yet to come.

I became worried when I sited an article titled: *"THE PATIENCE OF THE ELEPHANT AND THE ARROGANCE OF THE LION AND TIGER"*. When I perused the article, I became sad. Hence, the reason for writing this book **(THE BIASES OF**

THE ELEPHANT AGAINST THE LION AND LEOPARD) to educate all the Gbewaa Kingdom as one people from a common ancestor.

There is a saying in Dagbani: "A Tree on top of a hill does not cry for height but size". Although I am related to the legend's family of Bimbilla who hold oral tradition, I needed to grow, and the growth was from other sources. I am therefore indebted to the sources, which helped me to grow to my present height.

My initial source was oral tradition where I had to go from one person to another gathering data/information. Those who helped me in this were the following people: Alhaji Abdulai (Bimbilla Lung-Naa), Bagli Naa Mahama Wumbei Mahami, Namburugu Community Elders, Mohammed Awal Mahama (Kuglana), Mr. Inusah K. Dasoli, Vonaa Attah Abarika, Warikpamo Yahaya, Alhaji Braimah Damba (Bimbilla Tolon-Naa), Mr. Tia Robert Yakubu of Nalerigu Senior High School, Nayiri Bohagu II and his Elders and my elder brother, Alhaji Muhib Husein Kharma for the nice trip he arranged for me to visit Namburugu, not forgetting Nyong Lung-Naa Iddi Saaka.

Other sources from which I gathered my information were:

H. B. Martison, The Hidden History of Konkomba Wars in Northern Ghana

D. S$_T$J. –P, Legends of Northern Ghana.

Hizkias Assefa, Coexistence and Reconciliation in the Northern Region of Ghana.

Peter Skalnik, Chiefdom at War with Chiefless People while the Kingdom Looks on.

Ibrahim Mahama - History and Tradition of Dagbon, 2004.

Okyeame Ampadu-Agyei, A handbook on Totems in Ghana.

Cliff S. Maasole - The Konkomba and Their Neighbours.

The Northern Territories of The Gold Coast Under BritishColonial R u l e , 1897-1956:A S t u d y i n Political Change by Nana James Kwaku Brukum, 1997 (Unpublished).

I am very grateful to Mr. Adam Marshal (Forma Principal of Bimbilla E.P. Training College of Education and Historian) for editing this book. His contribution during the editing process has helped me to put the book into the desire sharp and content.

Many people have contributed to the production of the book whose names did not appear. To them I say Thank you.

Finally, I thank God (Almighty Allah) for the good health, time, and other resources he has granted me to produce this book.

Thank you.

Fusheini Yakubu

INTRODUCTION.

Mamprugu, Dagbon and Nanung are the three main sister states/kingdoms of Naa Gbewaa in Northern Ghana. The other sister state/kingdom is the Mossi Kingdom in Burkina Faso. The Builsa Chiefdom, Nabdan Chiefdom, Talensi Chiefdom, and the Waala Chiefdom are the other smaller states of Naa Gbewaa in Northern Ghana. These Gbewaa States are descendants of Naa Gbewaa and the Aboriginal Dagbamba who traced their origin to one ancestor's.

The sad story at stake, is when kingdoms from a common ancestor failed to leverage on each other's strengths and opportunities but rather begins to attack each other psychological or physical. According to oral literature by the late Bimbilla Lung-Naa Alhaj Abdulai 2008, as at the time the property of Naa Gbewaa and the "Nam" was going to be shared among the three great sons, Galinkuna Tohagu, Gmantambu and Nyagsi, son of Naa Sitobu. Galinkuna Tohagu was the elder. That is, after the death of Zirli, Kufogu, and Sitobu, Galinkuna Tohagu (Founder of Mamprugu Kingdom) was next as the elder. That is the reason, Mamprusis are the elders because the founder of Mamprugu Kingdom was the first to receive his share of the properties and the regalia of Naa Gbewaa "Nam". Naa Nyagsi, son of Sitobu was next and Naa Gmantambu (Founder of Nanung Kingdom) was third respectively at Namburugu "Nam Tariya Tuu-Gbuni", located in the present-day Karaga District. It is a historical fact, and nobody can take that away from Mamprusis. I became worried when I sited an article titled: *"THE PATIENCE OF THE ELEPHANT AND THE ARROGANCE OF THE LION AND TIGER"*. When I perused the article, I became sad. Hence, the reason for writing this book **(THE BIASES OF THE ELEPHANT AGAINST THE LION AND LEOPARD)** to educate all the Gbewaa Kingdom as one people from a common ancestor. The Elephant is the Totem of Mamprugu. The Lion is the Totem of Dagbon, and the Leopard is the Totem of Nanung. The arrogance of the lion and Tiger instead of Leopard is referring to Dagbon and Nanung by the author of the article: *"THE PATIENCE OF THE ELEPHANT AND THE ARROGANCE OF THE LION AND TIGER"*.

This book is not a counterattack on the previous article from elders of Mamprugu Kingdom but to provide accurate information on the evolution of the Gbewaa Kingdoms. Such that readers will appreciate the genealogy of the Gbewaa Kingdoms as one people with the same or similar cultural practices, custom and tradition.

DEDICATION.

I am dedicating this book to the great kings of the four main Gbewaa Kingdoms in Ghana and Burkina Faso, Mamprugu, Dagbon, Nanung and Mossi Kingdom. My dedication also goes to the following Gbewaa Chiefdoms: Builsa Chiefdom, Nabdan Chiefdom, Talensi Chiefdom and Waala Chiefdom. My special dedication goes to Nayiri Naa Bohagu II (Mahami Abdulai), Yaa Naa Abubakari Mahama II, Late Bimbilla Naa Dassana Abdulai and the late Bimbilla Naa Abarika Attah II.

My special dedication also goes to Africans in the Diaspora and the youth in the Gbewaa Kingdoms.

CHAPTER 1

1.0 OVERVIEW OF GBEWAA STATES.

1.1 "Tohazie" The Red Hunter

The history[11] of the Gbewaa States, which is referred to us by some writers as the Rulers of Great Dagbon, begins with the story of a man popularly known as "Tohazie" Red Hunter. Tohazie was the only son of Tiyawumya. Tiyawumya came from King Shabarko family of ancient Egypt. Tiyawumya was born in Massari. He moved to Thungi and from Thungi to Morocco. After some time, he later migrated to Chad and finally to Gomba (Zamfara) where he gave birth to Tohazie. Tohazie from Zamfara in Northern Nigeria moved to the Mali Empire. By his profession as a hunter in Mali, he killed a wild cow that had prevented the people of the village from having access to water, and thereby saved them from dying of thirst. With time, he became very popular and even led the people in war to defeat their enemies in the region. The King of Mali rewarded Tohazie for his services and bravery. The reward included a princess of Mali who was given to him as a wife by the King of Mali. Tohazie's wife was a lame woman called "Pag-wobga". It was believed that there might be something special about her. For, Tohazie chose her in preference to other princesses who had been paraded by the King of Mali. The issue of the Malian Princess and Tohazie was Kpogunumbo the wonderful being. According to oral tradition, Tohazie and his wife did not live to see the manhood of their son Kpogunumbo. They both died when he was still a child. Kpogunumbo grew up and inherited his father. He showed bravery similar to that of his father in wars between the Malians and their neighbours. He moved westward of the Mali Empire and finally arrived at Biun in Gruma land. Kpogunumbo succeeded the Fetish King of Biun in a fight and took over his kingdom, which he ruled until his death.

Naa Gbewaa who is the grandson of Kpogunumbo ascended to the throne after the death of Kpogunumbo. After some years in Biun, Naa Gbewaa migrated with a large following to Pusiga in the Upper East Region of Ghana near the Ghana- Togo border. He continued fighting the wicked Tindaanba from Pusiga to Yani-Dabari by a way of expanding chieftainship to promote good governance and democracy. Even though the Tindaanba had some form of governance systems in their communities, but it was not centrally coordinated. For the wicked Tindaanba, rule was like survival of the fittest that Naa Gbewaa was fighting. The wicked ones were killed, and new chiefs replaced to rule the communities and the obedient ones made chiefs of their communities. Naa Gbewaa did not fight and drive indigenous people away; rather they were integrated into the society. Some writers perceive Dagombas, Nanumbas and Mamprusi as war like people but that may be a wrong conclusion. Because the aboriginal Dagbamba were living together in harmony before the advent of the descendants of Naa Gbewaa, who came with force and introduced chieftainship in the three sister states of Great Dagbon. As such, Naa Gbewaa is regarded as the first King of Great Dagbon. Because Naa Gbewaa fought Tindaanba in a wide area, he was appellated as "Yogu -Tolana" meaning "warrior in a wide area". That is the reason why Yaa Naa, Nayiri of Mamprugu and Bimbilla Naa are also appellated as "Yogu -Tolana" because they are sons of Naa Gbewaa. Also, he was very powerful and the word "power" in Dagbani means "Yaa". The title Yaa Naa emanated from the powerful nature of Naa Gbewaa.

1.2 Naa Gbewaa Sons and Daughters.

Naa Gbewaa survived with a good number of children. According to some old school of oral tradition that Naa Gbewaa gave birth to nine children, others are of the view that the children were fifteen. Whatever it may be the most important thing is that, in his life, he gave birth to several children, but only seven (7) of them were very popular. First child was a female called Katchiogu (Pakpong Katchiogu: Ofa Nam Cheri) or Yentaure; named by French. It is based on this, they praise every Princess (Pakpong) "Katchiogu", next was Zirli, Kufogu, Sitobu (Sigri-Nitobu, Duri-ni Nam), Tohagu (Galinkuna Tohagu) and Gmantambu. Other children of Gbewaa included Kuhu-Naa Shebeei, Sinson Naa Buhuyeligu, Karaga-Lana Beimoni (he was the last born of Naa Gbewaa), Zantandana Yirigipeili and Yemo-Karaga Lana Karateili. Oral tradition could not tell how long Naa Gbewaa ruled Great Dagbon; one can only say that he ruled Great Dagbon for several years.

Zirli and Kufogu, due to leadership and power struggled over the succession of the kingship, fought each other and Zirli defeated Kufogu. The reason was because the first child of Naa-Gbewaa was a female and by the tradition, a female does not inherit the father's property. These two brothers being next to the female daughter (Katchiogu) resulted in a succession dispute. After Zirli defeated Kufogu, he also died shortly. The tragic death of these two sons led to the death of Naa Gbewaa, he went out at Yani-Dabari and mysteriously entered the ground somewhere around Pusiga in the Upper East Region of Ghana. A round room was built round to signify the grave of the Great King and can still be located there today. This marked the burial of the three Great Kings (Yaa Naa, Bimbilla Naa and Nayiri) in the local round rooms at their various palaces. Some writers and old school of oral tradition had it that, Zirili succeeded Naa Gbewaa. This may lead us to a great confusion. Zirili died shortly after he killed Kufogu. Sitobu (Sigri-Nitobu) was then the elder son of Naa-Gbewaa and ascended to the throne after the death of Naa Gbewaa. Sitobu got married and gave birth to Nyagsi. Nyagsi grew up.

1.3 The Leadership of Naa Sitobu.

One day, Sitobu secretly told Nyagsi (his first son) to go and meet his uncles and tell them to seek for fortification in terms of war from their elder brother 'Naa Sitobu'. The two uncles (Tohagu and Gmantambu) went to their elder brother "Naa Sitobu" and proposed it to him but were refuted by him. Some days later, Naa Sitobu again asked Nyagsi to go back to remind his uncles. Naa Sitobu refused once again, the third reminder was sent again. Now, Naa Sitobu agreed to the proposal, but expressed his concern on how Nyagsi was going to fight without support. Tohagu agreed to go with him. Gmantambu then suggested that half of them with the ammunitions remain at home to guide the king (Naa Sitobu) and the two of them would use the other half of ammunitions to accompany Nyagsi to fight. The king finally agreed and brought out the ammunitions "Tobri". Everything being equal, they started the war towards Gambaga and when they got to Gambaga, they met a well to do woman who was the "Tindana" and for that matter the Queen of Gambaga with some few ethnic groups namely, Mamprusis, Tamplensi, Kussasi and Bimobas. According to the descriptions by oral tradition, the woman was short in height, fair in complexion with red hair "Zabgu", very rich in terms of animals such as Cattle, Sheep, Goat, Poultry, Horses, Donkeys as well as cash (Cowries were used as legal tender for the payment of goods and services). The Queen gave Nyagsi with his warriors' a warm reception. In every three (3) days' time Nyagsi will demand 100 each of the animals and cash to an extent that Nyagsi depleted the Queen's wealth. One day Nyagsi again demanded as usual, the Queen sent a reply to Nyagsi that, all the animals together would not reach 100. Nyagsi still insisted. The Queen remarked that, "I knew very well, he is here to kill me, and I am not going anywhere; he should come and kill me". On that faithful Friday, Nyagsi got prepared and beheaded the Queen. Oral tradition stated, "The Queen did not sheer blood but milk". Those who saw that said, they have killed a blessed child of God, by then there were some few Muslims (Hausas) and these people rubbed their bodies with the milk to also get the blessing. Nyagsi said they should give him some of the milk to also rub his body. When Nyagsi applied the milk on his forehead, he developed mental illness. Tohagu and Gmantambu in their effort to get treatment for Nyagsi could not work after they went round the community's seeking treatment from elders (Herbalist/Spiritualist). Finally, they decided to send Nyagsi back home to the king (Naa-Sitobu) for treatment. On their way back, they got to Savelugu, and an elderly (Herbalist/Spiritualist) offered them some treatment and the sickness subsided. According to oral literature, the Herbalist/Spiritualist gave them between three to seven days to be discharged and before he was discharged, Nyagsi's hair was shaved. The very day he was discharged emanated Savelugu chieftainship and the practice of shaving people's hair at funerals for chiefs and elders "Kuzabri". By then Naa-Sitobu had moved from Yani-Dabarini to Bagli and sent a message to them, to meet him at Bagli where he was staying with the Bagli Tindana. When they got to Bagli, they met Naa-Sitobu at the Bagli Tindana's palace. Naa-Sitobu mandated his son that same day to ascend to the throne secretly in the night and mysteriously entered the ground. It is for this reason that Sitobu cursed the sons of Naa Gbewaa not to visit Bagli forever. Surprisingly, Tohagu and Gmantambu came the following morning to greet their elder brother "Naa-Sitobu", only to see Nyagsi in the Chief's Insignia. A succession dispute arose again between Nyagsi and his uncles (Tohagu & Gmantambu). They got angry and were going back to prepare, to fight Nyagsi. Nyagsi sent some elders to call his uncles back and they were directed through the back door of the Tindana's palace where their elder brother was buried. Hence, this is where it begins; the practice of passing through the back door by elders and sub-chiefs to see the grave of any of the three main Kings of the three sister states (Yaa-Naa, Bimbilla Naa & Nayiri) when any of them die.

1.4 Succession Dispute and the Partition of Gbewaa Kingdoms

Tohagu and Gmantambu got prepared to fight Nyagsi again after they realized, it was a planned thing, because by the tradition, they should have succeeded their elder brother (Naa-Sitobu) and groom Nyagsi but not Nyagsi to succeed his father (Naa-Sitobu). That was the reason why, they decided to fight and kill Nyagsi. Thank God, Bagli Tindana was a very good elderly person, who strongly intervened by directing them to proceed to Namburugu. When they got to Namburugu, they settled under a Baobab Tree. It was at this place the Bagli Tindana told them that it is at this place we are going to share your father's property to you. He told Naa Nyagsi that, your uncles knew their father's property and I in person knew about one of the properties that do not appear in a day light. It usually appears in the night and goes back in the night (the chief's insignia). For now, you have to produce all the properties that include Horses, Cattle, Sheep, Goat, Donkeys, Clothing, Money, Slaves and reserve the chief's insignia, tonight we will then finish the sharing. All the property was shared into three equal parts for the three of them. Tohagu, you are next to your brother Naa Sitobu, come and pick yours, followed by Sitobu elder son 'Nyagsi', you represent your father Naa Sitobu, take your property and Gmantambu also take yours. Nyagsi you cannot seize our legacy and include us. We should have inherited our father's legacy including you but what your father did to you we cannot disskinned you. The skins were also shared equally into three. Hence, Yaa Naa, Nayiri and Bimbilla Naa are sitting on the same Gbewaa Skins. Tonight, the chief's insignia were equally shared into three for them. For that matter, the same insignia are used to enskin Yaa Naa, Nayiri and Bimbilla Naa. It is important to note that, the sharing of Gbewaa Skin and properties was facilitated by Bagli Tindana and assisted by Salaa Tindana, Namburugu Tindana and other Sub-Tindaanba in the Bagli area. As such Bagli Tindana is the head of Tindaanba in the three sister Gbewaa states/kingdoms. Oral tradition states that, "the nature of the Insignia makes the three main kings to always move in the night for confidentiality".

When they got their shares of the property and the Insignia, they became powerful and said this was what our father used to fight and capture lands we will also do same. This led to the separation of the three Sister Gbewaa States into

Modern Dagbon, Mamprugu and Nanung. Tohagu took the direction of Mamprugu and settled at Mamprugu. Gmantambu headed towards Yeji through Salaga to Attebubu. As at then Salaga and Yeji were not in existence. The only settlement was Attebubu with temporal structures such as thatch. After Naa Gmantambu, the Hausa people through the Trans-Shara Trade sought permission from the Bimbilla Naa and settled in Salaga. Interestingly, these Gonjas from Kpembe/Salaga were refugees from West Gonja and they came and sought refuge from Bimbilla Naa. Bimbilla Naa accepted them and gave them Chirifa old settlement "Chirifa Dabari" to settle. They were farming vegetables such as Okro, Keneaf, etc. for Nanumbas and the few Hausa people who were there. This gave birth to the Kpembe Skin. It is important to note that Kpembe Skin Title originated from Nanung Kingdom.

Before they separated from each other at Namburugu, they took an oath of succession and equity that; they are all equal in titles; under no circumstances shall Yaa Naa enskin Bimbilla Naa or Nayiri and vice versa. This accounts for the reasons why princes from Dagbon, Mamprugu and Nanung forbid visiting Bagli community. Tong-Lana Yemusah, son of Naa Adan-Sigli, who attempted to break the record of "Bagli visit" mysteriously perished with his horse under a Baobab Tree that was closer to Bagli community. The Baobab Tree died in 2011. Moreover, this confirmed that, sons of Yaa Naa, Bimbilla Naa and Nayiri do not visit Bagli Community. Some writers and old school of oral tradition have it that, Mamprugu, Mossi and Modern Dagbon were founded between half of the 13th century to 14th century. What they failed to appreciate is the fact that, Naa Gbewaa ruled Great Dagbon (Modern Dagbon, Mamprugu and Nanung) for several years as one state. After the death of Naa Gbewaa and Naa Sitobu resulted in a succession dispute among Nyagsi and his uncles (Tohagu & Gmantambu) that they separated at the same time at Namburugu and founded their individual states/ kingdoms and is today regarded as sister states/kingdoms of Naa Gbewaa. Hence, as to whether the founding of Modern Dagbon and Mamprugu came after Nanung may lead us to the realm of speculation rather than of fact. Below are pictures of Namburugu community.

Namburugu (A Historic Community of Great Dagbon)

Namburugu Community Showing the Spot where the Gbewaa Skin Titles "Nam" were Shared Among the three Great Sons of Naa Gbewaa (Nam Tariya Tuu-Gbuni).

The spot in the ancient times was sited with a very big Baobab Tree. The Tree died several years ago and currently with a grove of Nim Trees. The stones on which they sat and shared the property are available today under the grove. Nevertheless, Namburugu community still has many Baobab Trees today to justify the presence of Baobab Tree at the spot in the ancient times.

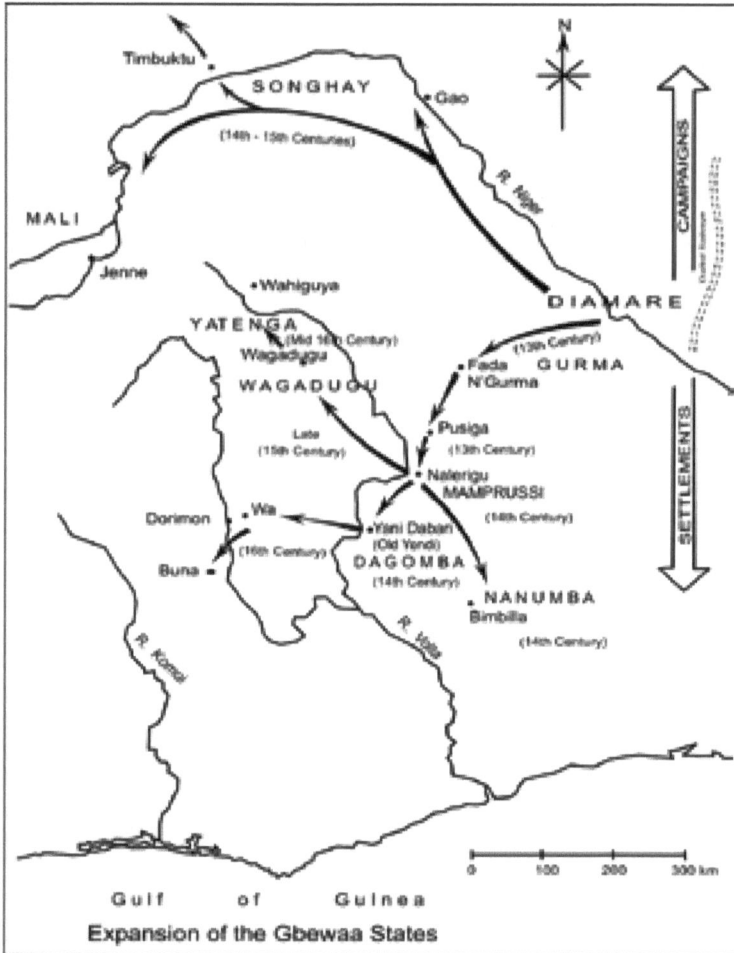

Fig. 3

CHAPTER 2

THE BIASES OF THE ELEPHANT AGAINST THE LION AND LEOPARD

According to author of the article (**THE PATIENCE OF THE ELEPHANT AND THE ARROGANCE OF THE LION AND TIGER**) "It is not for fun that when the Children of the Great Naa Gbewaa split to form the tripartite Kingdoms thus Mamprugu, Dagbong and Nanung and they decided to choose among the wildlife animals that would depict their nature, the Mamprusi depict the symbol Elephant, Yooba (Dagombas) picked the symbol Lion whiles Nanumbas choose the symbol Tiger". I would like to bring to his attention that the right term to use is Totem and not symbol as he applied in his grama. Totem is defined by Oxford Dictionary as "A natural object or animal that is believed by a particular society to have spiritual significance and that is adopted by it as an emblem". Also, "A person or thing regarded as being symbolic or representative of a particular quality or concept".

The author also lied by holding to the fact that the totem for Nanung is a Tiger. The totem for Nanung is a leopard and not a Tiger. He can refer to the Northern Regional House Chiefs and a Handbook on Totems in Ghana by Okyeame Ampadu-Agyei for confirmation. The totem "Leopard" symbolizes how fearless and worries Nanumbas are in fighting.

Again, the author holds as facts that "Tohugu, the eldest among Naa Gbewaa children and the grandfather of Mamprusi asked his Younger brother Sitobu the grandfather of Yoobas (Dagombas) to cross the White Volta and establish his Kingdom in the Yoo (Forest) which gave them the name Yooba. And point his hand (Nuu) at a certain direction and asked one of his younger brothers Gmantambu the grandfather of Nanumbas to establish his Kingdom there hence the name Nanung (Naa Nuu-Kings Hand)". These are more of speculations than historical facts.

Sitobu was the elder followed by Tohagu. Naa Gbewaa survived with a good number of children. According to some old school of oral tradition that Naa Gbewaa gave birth to nine children, others are of the view that the children were fifteen. Whatever it may be the most important thing is that, in his life, he gave birth to several children, but only seven (7) of them were very popular. First child was a female called Katchiogu (Pakpong Katchiogu: Ofa Nam Cheri) or Yentaure; named by French. It is based on this, they praise every Princess (Pakpong) "Katchiogu", next was Zirli, Kufogu, Sitobu "Sigri-Nitobu, Duri-ni Nam", Tohagu (Galinkuna Tohagu) and Gmantambu. Other children of Naa Gbewaa included Kuhu-Naa Shebeei, Sinson Naa Buhuyeligu, Karaga-Lana Beimoni (he was the last born of Naa Gbewaa), Zantandana Yirigipeili and Yemo-Karaga Lana Karateili.

It is important to put on record that after the death of Sitobu resulted in the succession dispute and the partition of the Gbewaa Kingdoms. As such, Bagli Tindana facilitated the resolution of the succession dispute and the partition of the Gbewaa Kingdoms. I humbly suggest to the Author, Badigamsira Inusah Abdul-Majeed to conduct further research to update his article (**THE PATIENCE OF THE ELEPHANT AND THE ARROGANCE OF THE LION AND TIGER**).

Furthermore, he claimed that "Nayiri point his hand (Nuu)

at a certain direction and asked one of his younger brothers Gmantambu the grandfather of Nanumbas to establish his Kingdom there hence the name Nanung (Naa Nuu-Kings Hand)". This is more a rumour than historical fact.

The ethnic name "Nanumba" is a corrupted Nawuri statement, whenever Naa Gmantambu invites the Nawuris to a meeting in Bimbilla. They do make this statement in the ancient times; "Naa Nuba" meaning, "Go and hear and come". In those days, only few of the Nawuris could speak Dagbani/Nanunli, so those who understand the language were always chosen to attend meetings of Naa Gmantambu. After which they will go back home and passed the information to the others. The long stay of Nanumbas with Nawuris, as well as inter-marriages corrupted the original Dagbani that was spoken by the aboriginal Dagbamba to the present-day Nanunli dialect.

The partition of the Gbewaa Kingdoms did not happen out of fun or peace and harmony but as a result of a succession dispute at Bagli in 1400. The rhetorical question is, who would have waited for the other to ask him to cross the White Volta or point his hand at a certain direction to go and establish their kingdoms? It is on record that the partition of the Gbewaa Kingdoms into three was as a result of a succession dispute like what we are experiencing today in some of the Gbewaa Kingdoms.

More so, the author holds as historical facts "The King of Mamprugu was named NaYiri (Naam Yiri) meaning he is the embodiment of Royalty and is the home for the Yooba (Dagombas) and Nanumba". It is more of a shopping list of speculations than historical facts. The kingdom was one during the reign of Naa Gbewaa and Naa Sitobu. The succession dispute arose when Naa Sitobu Mandated his son, Naa Nyagsi and mysteriously entered the ground at the Bagli Tindana's Palace in

1400. The succession dispute led to the partition of the Gbewaa Kingdoms and they parted at "Namburugu Nam Tariya Tuu-Gbuni" after they received their share of Naa Gbewaa property and the Insignia. The question again is, how did it become a home for Yooba (Dagombas) and Nanumba. Mamprusi called it Nayiri because that is their traditional headquarters and the seat of the king of Mamprugu Kingdom. The spelling and pronunciation "Nayiri" is in the Mamprungli dialect. If it was a home for both Yooba and Nanumba, the name would have been unique to represent as Gbewaa represent all the kingdoms. Yooba (Dagombas) and Nanumbas called it "Nayili" meaning chief's palace.

Narrating the biases of the Elephant, the author further indicated "a covenant was made at this juncture that, whenever a Dagomba or a Nanung have an issue, they should come to Mamprugu and should a Mamprusi also have issues they should consult Dagombas and/or Nanumbas. This was primarily evidenced when the Dagombas had civil war with the Gonjas during the era of Naa Darizegu and was defeated with Naa Darizigu killed at the war leading to the displacement of their administrative capital from Yani-Dabari (Diare) to Yendi. Naa Luro upon succeeding the skins of Yani seek refuge from the NaYiri and Mamprugu and later on wage war with the Gonjas and reclaimed victory". I am very surprised and wondering where the author got these speculations. During the reign of Naa Dariziegu and Naa Luro, the traditional administrative headquarters and seat of the king of Dagbon was at Yani-Dabari. The war between Naa Dariziegu and Gonjas was fought on Gonja Land and not on Dagbon Land. The same as that of Naa Luro. It was during the reign of Naa Tituguri (Zuu Tituguri), son of Naa Luro, the administrative capital of Dagbon was relocated to the present-day Yendi due to war between Naa Tituguri and the Gonjas.

Naa Luro regent (Zuu Titugri) also remained on the skin as Yaa Naa. It was then the Gonjas mobilized forces to attack Naa Titugri with the reason being that there was confusion among Dagbon chiefs and for that matter when they attack Naa Titugri, the other chiefs will not support him in the fight. As such, their chances of conquering him will be high and if they conquer him, it means they have conquered the whole Dagbon. Indeed, they attacked Naa Titugri (Zuu Titugri) and no chief from Dagbon supported him in the fight against the Gonjas. Until Bimbilla Naa sent tropes to help him fight them, off. From then Yani was moved from Yani-Dabari to the current Yendi, based on the advice from Bimbilla Naa to settle closer to him so that he can easily give him support when the need arises, "because you are far away from me". Bimbilla Naa indicated to him that, he has conquered his side, and no one can attempt him. Naa Titugri (Zuu Titugri) was the one who moved Yani from Yani-Dabari to the current Yani (Yendi).

When he moved to the current Yani, Bimbilla Naa felt the land was too small for him and gave the current Mion (Saambu) and Kpabya area to Naa Titugri and he enskinned his younger brother 'Voli' as Mion Lana. Hence, Mion Lana Voli was the first chief of Mion in Dagbon. The old Mion is the one in Jagbuni in Nanung Kingdom. The current Mion and Kpabya area was owned by the Jagbuni (Mion) Tindana.

The historical fact is that Tohagu was the eldest son of Naa Gbewaa during the resolution of the succession dispute and the partition of Gbewaa Kingdoms at "Namburugu Nam Tariya Tuu-Gbuni" which was facilitated by Bagli Tindana and assisted by Namburugu Tindana, among others. It is for this reason Mamprusis emerged as the elders. However, the Skin Titles "Nam" are equal. An oath was sworn by the three sons. For more information refer to the above heading: Overview of the Gbewaa Kingdoms, sub-heading, Succession Dispute, and the Partition of Gbewaa Kingdoms.

According to the author, "after the demise of Yaa Naa Gungobli (Wumbei) there was a feared competition as to who should be enskinned as Yaa Naa. The king makers upon realizing there could be conflict, seek help from the then NaYiri (Naa Atabiya) and Naa Zangina was enskinned peacefully". I perfectly agree with these as historical facts and the effort of Nayiri (Naa Atabiya) on his role as a Sole Mediator during the trying times of Dagbon chieftaincy succession crisis. The author should have been writing on these important historical events that will foster unity among the Gbewaa Kingdoms the author is of the view that "for over Eight (8) Centuries the NaYiri have always acted as the Elephant that he is. Thus, anywhere he goes Peace prevails. It is well known that the Elephant is an herbivore and does not cause any harm to other inhabitants of the jungle but rather serve as refuge to inhabitants whose lives are under threat". I think the author did not understand the totem of Mamprugu Kingdom. The totem of Mamprugu (Elephant) is a symbol of authority. Damba, a festival which is celebrated annually, is reverence for the totem (Elephant). Elephants are endangered because of the activities of poachers in the traditional area. They, however, occur occasionally around the Gambaga Scarp.

The author further holds as historical facts that "the Lion on the other hand is a carnivore and feed on only flesh and will feed on anything when it is hungry. When the Lion is hungry, it will even feed on its very own. Animals whose lives have been threaten by the Lion often seek refuge from the Elephant". The author's interpretation of the totem of Dagbon (Lion) is either mischievous or did not understand what the Lion represent. The totem of Dagbon (Lion) symbolizes how Dagombas fight fiercely like lions. The Yaa Naa sit on Lion skins including other wild animals' skins as the king of Dagbon.

The author holds grievance "the NaYiri have been a peace mediator for the past centuries and will always be. Thus he (NaYiri) is not perturbed by the current posture of the Dagombas in their bit to sabotage to creation of the North East Region. But let it be known to them that the Capital of Northern territory in the Precolonial era was moved from Gambaga to Tamale and Mamprusi saw nothing wrong with that because we thought we were brothers". The author should get it right that Dagombas were not in any way against the creation of North East Region. They were concerned with Cheriponi being caved out from Northern Region to North East Region. It is a known fact by all that Cheriponi is under Dagbon Traditional Council. No traditional leader will look on for some part of his/ her traditional area to be taken away.

On the relocation of the administrative capital of Northern Territory from Gambaga to Tamale, was not the influence of Dagombas. The administration of Northern Territories was established at Gambaga by our colonial masters in 1896 to 1906. The administration lasted for a decade after which they thought it prudent and relocated the administration to Tamale in 1906. The reason for the relocation was for quicker communication with both the south and north than the former which was in the north-eastern corner of the territory. It is important to note that the administration of Northern Territories was established at Gambaga by our colonial masters and later relocated the administration to Tamale by the same colonial masters.

The author tagged Nanumbas, like Dagombas as arrogance but could not prove the wrongdoing of Nanumbas. Is it because Mamprusis are elders and can at any time rain insults on any of the other Gbewaa Kingdoms? Hmmm. The author should apologies to Nanumbas.

2.1 Recommendations.

We should write on historical events that will foster unity among the three Gbewaa sister kingdoms and the related chiefdoms.

An annual durbar of chiefs for the four Gbewaa Kingdoms in Ghana and Burkina Faso and the other related chiefdoms should be instituted. The durbar should be organized on rotational basis.

Mamprugu Kingdom should develop a very good strategic plan to market their kingdom to the world for a very good exposure.

A common website should be developed to showcase the culture, custom and tradition of the Gbewaa Kingdoms to the world. I' Fusheini Yakubu has taken the lead and contracted a consultant to develop the website. It is at the developing stage.

CHAPTER 3

THE ADMINISTRATION OF NORTHERN TERRITORIES OF THE GOLD COAST.

According to the Order in Council of 1902, the area which became known as the Northern Territories of the Gold Coast was constituted[40]. This was after the Anglo-French and Anglo-German conventions of 1898 and 1899 respectively which defined their various boundaries. Even before the conclusion of the agreements, in 1897 the Northern Territories were divided into three districts centered on Kintarnpo, Wa and Garnbaga under a scheme submitted by Lt. Col. Northcott, the first Commissioner and Commander. The Northern Territories were divided into the Black Volta, White Volta and Kintampo districts. The first two were subdivided into seven subdistricts of Dagarti, Grunshi, Frafra, Mamprusi, Wa, Bole and Daboya. The main principles which guided the definition of the subdistricts were as follows:

a) the successful administration, "pacification" and development of these territories was dependent upon the ubiquity of the white man[11].

b) the subdistricts could "be capable from their size, of being effectively regulated by an European"

> c) the boundaries should adhere as nearly as possible
> to the existing racial boundaries.

The period preceding the advent of British rule witnessed the destruction and exhaustion of both human and material resources of the country through war and slave raiding. The area between Wain North-West, latitude 11 to the North and Mamprugu to the east and North-Est was occupied by non-centralized people such as Kasem, Isala, Kusasi, Builsa and Frafra. Their area was the hunting grounds for slaves by Babatu and Samori. Life was therefore uncertain, the people were suspicious of all strangers, and the disturbed conditions discouraged both trade and agriculture. This made it impossible for them to resist any foreign conqueror although the Frafra made some uncoordinated attempts to resist the British. Consequently, after the British occupation of the area, the most pressing problem was the restoration of peace. For the effective control and uniform development of the country, the administrative units had to be compact and limited in area. The coincidence of ethnic and administrative boundaries, if these were possible, would have the double advantage of avoiding the possibility of conflict with the authorities of the various chiefs and ensuring ethnic uniformity and hence a higher degree of cooperation with administrative areas. Support for the authority of the chiefs was recognized early as the only practical and economic way for the effective control and rapid development of this large tract of territory.

The push to the interior and the attendant military operations shifted the centre of gravity of the disputed territory further north. The expediency of acting promptly at a distance from the headquarters, as well as the necessity for rapid communication with the scattered detachments to facilitate concentration of energies, underlined the importance of the Officer Commanding being brought closer to the area of active confrontation. So, from December 1897, Gambaga became for all practical purposes, the seat of the Commissioner and Commander of the Northern Territories, formally superseding Kintarnpo, as the headquarters in July 1898. Also, in 1902, the 1898 administrative arrangements were abolished by the creation of new administrative areas. This was in conformity with the rival scheme submitted by Governor Hodgson. Although the title and headquarters of the three divisions were retained with considerable modifications effected in their boundaries. A new administrative unit, the Gonja district was established with Salaga as its headquarters. Although the 1898 Northcott arrangements had been accepted as the basis for the administration of the Northern Territories, the establishment was chronically short of its complement of officers, essentially because of the difficulties of obtaining military personnel of the right caliber. The South African War of 1899 further depleted the staff serving in those territories, while the Asante Rebellion of 1900[42] not only prevented officers from proceeding to the North but focused attention on Asante.

The year 1907 marked an important step in the history of the Northern Territories. In that year the military administration was replaced by a civilian regime mainly because it was apparent that the military administration was inadequate for effective governance. Although the three main divisions still existed, Tamale and not Kintampo became the headquarters of the Southern province. A year later the headquarters of the Northern Territories was transferred from Gambaga to Tamale because the latter was centrally placed and afforded a quicker communication with both the south and north than the former which was in the north-eastern corner of the territory. These territorial arrangements remained until 1921 when the number of provinces was reduced to two mainly for economic reasons. However, with the introduction of indirect rule in 1930, the three provinces were re-established this time, with Navrongo and not Gambaga as headquarters of the North-Eastern Province. This arrangement remained in place until 1960.

First, the British turned the area into a labour pool for the rest of the country. In this connection no efforts were made to develop the economic potential of the area neither was the infrastructure developed except the few "political roads". Recruitment of people for the mines, railway construction, army and police was seen as the North's only contribution to national development. Efforts were also made to isolate the area from the rest of the country. To implement this policy, western education and its main agent, the mission were to be restricted in the North. To prevent what was regarded as the "untoward influence" of education, and again to prevent the southern virus from contaminating the innocent northern, indirect rule was introduced and strengthened from 1935.

In West Africa, British colonial administrators worked on the assumption that they could reform traditional institutions to conform with western models. The role of the colonial power was to rule until such a time as the indigenous people could prove themselves capable of self-governance in European (preferably British) fashion. The duty of the colonial officials also included the provision of instruments whereby colonial people could acquire the skills necessary for good governance. For many officials, the most important such instrument was the system of indirect rule defined by one former colonial official as governing local affair through the customary institutions of the people of the area. For the British indirect rule was truly ingenious as an instrument of colonial administration, as a precursor of self-government, however, this was ruin. It had two main weaknesses, the period it presumed and its assumptions as to who was to rule. According to Sir Andrew Cohen *"the method of applying indirect rule was based on the assumption that we had an indefinite time ahead which the system could grow and develop under our guidance"*.

However, after 1945, it became clear that the unlimited period on which the colonial rule rested was no longer valid, nor were the practice which promoted traditional elements over the small but westernized elite which evolved. Thus, one of the first casualties of the increased pace of change after the Second World War, was indirect rule. In its place, the British attempted to implant a system of government modelled on that at home. At the level of colony-wide institutions, changes were introduced to transform legislative and executive councils into parliaments and cabinet respectively along Westminster lines. This was the unfortunate situation the Northern Territories found itself after 1951. The nature of the colonial economy pursued, the distribution of social services particularly education, the organization of the colonial administration and in some cases even the predisposition of some colonial officials created an irregular rate of change in the Gold Coast. Hitherto from 1951, all parts of the Gold Coast were supposed to march together towards imminent nationhood. One result of this was that the Northern Territories which had "lagged behind" in socio-economic development were pushed forward at an extremely rapid pace; political change was artificially induced or even imposed. It responded by emphasizing regional particularities and resisted attempts to be dominated by the more advanced Asante and the Gold Coast Colony. But it fought in vain. Reluctantly, on 6th March 1957, the Northern Territories joined the rest of the country in nationhood.

CHAPTER FOUR

4.0 SLAVE TRADE AND ITS RESISTANCE IN THE GBEWAA KINGDOMS.

4.1 Transatlantic Slave Trade.

Cape Coast which is located on the shore of the Atlantic Ocean and the Cape Coast Castle was one of the last points of contact for the enslaved Africans before they were taken away from the continent to work on the plantations of the New World[6].

When it comes to making slave-trade heritage, Northern Ghana towns such as, Paga have a lot to offer. Beyond the subliminal spiritual significance of the pilgrimage lies the economic potential. Northern Ghana's linkage with the Transatlantic slave trade is too strong to be taken lightly. From Sandema to Yendi, Gwollu to Nalerigu the landscape is replete with relics. (Akpabli 2001).

Figure 1Salaga Slave Wells & Bath where Slaves were Bathed.

What is striking in this statement is the fact that all the sites that are mentioned, including the Pikworo Slave Camp at Paga, Saakpuli Slave Market, Salaga Slave Market, Salaga Slave Wells & Bath, Juole Defense-Wall are primarily connected to the slave raids of the Zabarima traders, Babatu and Samori in the late nineteenth century. By that time, the transatlantic slave trade had already been abolished for a few decades; the British slave trade activity officially ceased in 1807, France followed in 1848, and Brazil, which was reluctant to abolish the lucrative business, was forced to do so in 1852. Even though the official abolition did not lead to a complete halt in slaving activities but rather in an increase in illegal slave exports in some areas, the eventual ending of the institution of slavery in the Americas also marked the end of the transatlantic slave trade[11]. In the British colonies, this was done in 1834, in the United States in 1865 and finally in Brazil in 1888. By then the industrial revolution had changed the face of Euro-American economy and the major European powers began their scramble for Africa in order to facilitate direct colonial exploitation. However, the inner-African and indigenous slave trade went on for a longer period. In Asante and the Northern territories of the Gold Coast, laws on the emancipation of slaves were passed as late as 1908, institution of slavery still operating illegally at least up to 1928 (cf Perbi 2002: 193 – 205).

Figure 2: Salaga Slave Market - Captured Slaves were Chained onto this Baobab Tree.

Although the slave sites in Northern Ghana are primarily related to the slave raids of the late nineteenth century, the earlier transatlantic slave trade had made impact here, too. Mossi and Hausa traders operated in those areas long before Babatu and Samori entered the historical stage (cf Der 1998).

4.2 Resistance of Slave Trade in Northern Ghana By Traditional Rulers.

Before the passage of law in 1908, traditional rulers in the Gbewaa Kingdoms resisted slave activities by Babatu and Samori among others by fighting them. This led to a war between Dagombas and Zabarima people in the present-day Niger. The war was resolved by the signing of peace treaty between Dagombas and Zabarimas. This paved a way for the Babatu and Samori continue their slave trade in the Non-Gbewaa Kingdoms. In the light of this, Bolga and Bongo joined the Gbewaa Kingdoms to be freed from Babatu and Samori slave activities. The Builsa people finally defeated Babatu and Samori in a war between the Builsa and the Slave Traders (Babatu and Samori). They took their weapons and dumped them under a Tree. The spot has become a shrine in the Builsa land and annual rituals are performed there to mark their success over the Zabarima slave raiders. Babatu did not returned to his home country but rather went and settled in Yendi and that was where he retired from slave trade. The grave of Babatu can still be found in Yendi with the slave chains and shackles.

Figure 3: Babatu Grave at Yendi

The construction of slave defense walls at Gwollu, Nalerigu (built with milk & human parts) and Juole were part of the efforts explored by traditional rulers to resist the activities of slave trade in Northern Ghana.

Figure 4: Defense Wall at Gwollu

Figure 5: Defense Wall at Nalerigu

4.3 Conclusion.

Africans were themselves capturing their fellow Africans as slaves to the Whiteman and seen as a lucrative business without considering the negative impact.

Africans in the diaspora can be traced to the United State of America and Europe. The question I could not find answer to, is Africans who were enslaved and exported to the Arabian. Where are they today or where can we find them?

There was intra African slave trade or indigenous slave trade. Since the laws on the emancipation of slaves were passed as late as 1908. By 1930s slaves were integrated in the society. Today in Northern Ghana, one cannot trace who was a slave in this modern society.

Slave trade had been abolished and Africa has gained independence from our colonial masters. The rhetorical question, is Africa totally free from the Whiteman? The answer is no, because Africa gained only physical independence and psychologically African leaders have been remoted by the white man. Until we emancipate ourselves from mental slavery before we can gain psychological independence from the Whiteman.

Psychological independence is the key to Africa socio-economic development. Africa has a population of 1.2 billion which is very good for market attraction. The sad news is that Africa is performing less than 17% for trade among Africans (Ghana National Export Development Strategy, 2020).

African leaders have initiated African Continental Free Trade Area (AFCFTA). 54 out 55 countries have signed except Eritrea. This initiative is to boost trade among Africans. The head office is located in Accra, Ghana. AFCFTA is scheduled to start in 2021.

The number of slave sites in Northern Ghana is a clear justification that most African Diasporas came from Northern Ghana and not the Southern Part of Ghana. Cape Coast which is located on the shore of the Atlantic Ocean and the Cape Coast Castle was one of the last points of contact for the enslaved Africans and not their origins.

BIBLIOGRAPHY.

A handbook on Totems in Ghana by Okyeame Ampadu-Agyei.

Accra Declaration. 1995 on the WTO-UNESCO Cultural Tourism Programme "The Slave Route, 4th April 1995, Accra, Ghana, Adopted on 29th April 1995, in Durban, South Africa, by the 27th meeting of the Regional Commission for Africa of the World Tourism Organization, Paris, UNESCO.

Akpabli, K. 2001. A Pilgrimage to Paga; The Tourist November 2001: N.P.

Bimbilla Lung-Naa, oral Literature source, 2008.

Cliff S. Maasole - The Konkomba and Their Neighbours.

Der, B. G. 1998. The Slave Trade in Northern Ghana. Accra: Woeli.

Fusheini Yakubu, History of the Gbewaa States – Part I, New Edition, 2013.

Featured Article by Fusheini Yakubu, Slave Trade and Its Resistance in the Gbewaa States, 27th November 2020.

Ghana National Export Development Strategy, 2020.

H. B. Martison, The Hidden History of Konkomba Wars in Northern Ghana.

Hizkias Assefa, Coexistence and Reconciliation in the Northern Region of Ghana.

Ibrahim Mahama - History and Tradition of Dagbon, 2004.

Oxford English Dictionary.

Rattray, R. S. 1932. The Tribes of the Ashanti Hinterland, 2 vols. (Oxford: Clarendon Press' repr. 1969).

Shinnie, P. and P. Ozanne. 1972 Excavation at Yani Dabari' Transactions of the Historical Society of Ghana No. 6.

Slave Route Projects: Tracing the Heritage of Slavery in Ghana. Article by Katharina Schramm, University of Bayreuth, 2008.

Tamakloe, E. F. 1931 A Brief History of the Dagbamba People (Accra, Government Printer).

The Northern Territories of The Gold Coast Under BritishColonial R u l e , 1897-1956:A S t u d y i n Political Change by Nana James Kwaku Brukum, 1997 (Unpublished).

The Patience of the Elephant and the Arrogance of the Lion and Tiger, an Article by Badigamsira Inusah Abdul-Majeed, 2020.

www.ingramcontent.com/pod-product-compliance
Lightning Source LLC
Chambersburg PA
CBHW040938030426
42335CB00001B/31